COMMON SOLUTIONS
for the
UNCOMMON CHILD

COMMON SOLUTIONS
for the
UNCOMMON CHILD

by

KIMBERLEY HAAG

KEITH KASPER

ELIZABETH DZIAK KRYST

EDITH YOUNG

Illustrated by

DAN PITKIN

ORDER FROM
KIDSRIGHTS
10100 Park Cedar Drive, Charlotte, NC 28210
1-800/892-KIDS, 704/541-0100, Fax 704/541-0113

COMMON SOLUTIONS for the UNCOMMON CHILD

Published by KIDSRIGHTS
        10100 Park Cedar Drive
        Charlotte, NC 28210
        (704) 541-0100

10 9 8 7 6 5 4
Forth Printing

ISBN: 1-55864-008-8

Table of Contents

INTRODUCTION

The profession of teaching can be a satisfying and rewarding experience. The goal of educating and enriching a child's mind is a stimulating challenge willingly accepted by those in the profession. However, in these times of budget cuts and inadequate funding, more is demanded of the classroom teacher. More and more pressure is put on schools and teachers to be accountable not only for educating but also for requiring students to master basic competency and survival skills.

The dedicated teacher struggles to provide the best education for the individual child. This can become frustrating and require a great deal of time to reflect and readjust. The challenge is compounded further when some of the students have exceptional needs. Since the passage of P.L. 94-142, teachers are finding special education students in their classrooms for at least part of the day. These mainstreamed students have a multitude of functioning levels and needs, and they require some academic and/or behavioral assistance beyond the needs of other students. This book was prepared for regular education teachers who have these exceptional students in the classroom.

Although each special child has individual needs, working with these students has revealed that many have similar deficiencies but to varying degrees, and with some overlap. General profiles were developed because of these universal traits. Each profile has a name, a face, and a general description as well as a list of characteristic behavior.

A teacher who observes a particular behavior by a student can locate the behavior on the characteristics list. Next to the behavior are numbers for suggested strategies located in the latter part of the book. These strategies are actual techniques that have been used and that the regular education teacher can implement without devoting a great deal of time to a particular student. It is intended that more strategies be suggested than will be used. Only the ones that are consistent with and complementary to the teacher's style of teaching need be employed.

The information in this book can be used with great diversity. It is a guide for the new teacher as well as the experienced teacher. It is a means for discussing a student by referring to a profile, thus maintaining confidentiality. This information may also serve as an inservice to prepare and inform regular education teachers about the special education children in their classes and about various ways of working with them.

Common Solutions for the Uncommon Child (K – 4)

The 14 profiles in the kindergarten through fourth grade section provide characteristic behavior of students with specific learning disabilities and/or behavior disorders. It is intended that students in the lower grades with these traits receive some sort of remedial help in overcoming these deficiencies as well as in utilizing their strengths in the classroom.

STEVIE SQUIRMER

Profile

I. STEVIE SQUIRMER – The "active" child

CHARACTERISTICS	STRATEGIES
a. Cannot sit still in his seat	1, 18, 35, 66, 128, 131
b. Often has part of his body in the aisle, or on top of the desk	1, 18, 35, 66, 128, 131
c. Generally has shoes untied or completely off, pants often not completely fastened	18, 35, 82, 129, 131
d. Is out of his seat every other minute	1, 18, 35, 59, 62, 65, 66, 85, 118, 128, 130, 131, 132
e. Needs the teacher's attention constantly; often screams the teacher's name across the room	1, 18, 22, 23, 24, 35, 59, 62, 65, 85, 112, 118, 128, 131, 132
f. Seldom faces forwards in his seat	1, 18, 35, 59, 62, 65, 85, 112, 128, 131
g. Usually is distracting to other students, sometimes unconsciously	1, 18, 35, 59, 60, 62, 70, 111, 112, 114, 118, 128, 131, 132
h. Pokes people in line, puts his feet on others' desks	1, 18, 35, 59, 62, 65, 67, 70, 111, 112, 113, 118, 131, 132
i. Uses negative behavior to get attention	1, 23, 29, 59, 60, 61, 62, 63, 64, 65, 66, 67, 85, 111, 112, 115, 118
j. Picks fights	1, 2, 9, 60, 61, 62, 63, 65, 66, 67, 70, 85, 112, 113, 132
k. Is the class clown	1, 29, 59, 60, 61, 62, 63, 64, 65, 66, 67, 70, 85, 97, 111, 112, 113, 114, 118
l. Seldom completes a total assignment	23, 35, 41, 42, 51, 55, 62, 74, 81, 84, 97, 106
m. Usually needs to have directions repeated	2, 6, 195, 199

SARAH SILENT

Profile

II. SARAH SILENT – The withdrawn child

CHARACTERISTICS	STRATEGIES
a. Seldom speaks	25, 28, 61, 134, 135, 138, 145, 146, 147, 154, 169, 170, 172
b. Often won't speak when spoken to	25, 26, 61, 135, 138, 146, 147, 169, 170
c. May just stare when spoken to	25, 26, 61, 135, 138, 147, 154, 170, 199
d. Won't participate in show and tell	18, 139, 147, 171
e. Is painfully shy, withdrawn	25, 26, 96, 133, 135, 138, 139, 146, 147, 154, 170, 193
f. Seems slow academically	2, 15, 22, 43, 52, 97, 105, 109, 125, 172, 173, 174
g. Is neither liked nor disliked by other children – they tolerate her	134, 138, 139, 154
h. Touches the wall and looks downward when walking down the hall	18, 29, 35, 147, 169
i. Resists physical contact	137, 154
j. Has a difficult time with change or new things	2, 43, 105, 109, 125
k. Is afraid to speak up in class even if her answer is correct	18, 25, 26, 35, 116, 170, 171, 172

9

Profile

III. CLUMSY CHARLIE – The child with gross motor coordination difficulties

CHARACTERISTICS	STRATEGIES
a. Can't jump rope or skip	148, 150, 151, 152, 167, 175
b. Walks with a special gait	148, 149, 150, 151, 152, 175
c. Falls off his chair or seat	18, 35, 148, 150, 151, 152, 175
d. Bumps into people and things	18, 35, 148, 149, 150, 151, 152, 175
e. Spills milk, drops food	18, 35, 148, 149, 150, 151, 152
f. Knocks down desks and chairs	18, 35, 148, 149, 150, 151, 152, 175
g. Is unable to catch or throw a ball	148, 150, 151, 152, 167, 175
h. Is unable to follow simple rhythm activities	148, 150, 151, 152, 167, 175
i. May be overweight	18, 150, 175
j. Has trouble in P.E.	148, 152, 175

Profile

IV. NEAL KNOW-IT-ALL – The child who is unrealistic about his abilities and inabilities

CHARACTERISTICS	STRATEGIES
a. Says everything is "easy"	2, 59, 60, 85, 112, 118, 132, 136, 153
b. Will quickly say, "Oh, I know how to do that," to any new thing	2, 59, 60, 85, 112, 118, 132, 136, 153
c. May have been retained, and may feel bad about it	136, 153
d. Always wants to be in the hardest book and may take out library books well above his reading level	38, 85, 86, 132, 136, 153, 194, 198, 199
e. Grimaces and groans about anything new presented, including art, music, P.E.	59, 60, 65, 67, 85, 86, 132, 136, 153
f. Often doesn't finish assignments	2, 38, 41, 42, 43, 51, 54, 65, 74, 81, 86, 87, 102, 108, 109, 192
g. Says he is finished with an assignment but isn't	4, 6, 23, 38, 42, 43, 51, 54, 65, 69, 74, 81, 86, 102, 108, 109, 194
h. Generally is careless with any assignment	1, 2, 4, 20, 23, 37, 38, 43, 44, 47, 51, 52, 53, 54, 55, 57, 58, 65, 79, 81, 86, 87, 97, 109, 192
i. Consistently hands in incorrect assignments and incorrect corrections	15, 20, 23, 37, 51, 52, 53, 54, 55, 56, 57, 58, 79, 81, 86, 97, 105, 109, 123, 192
j. Gives illogical verbal and written answers	7, 43, 51, 97, 109, 123, 124, 171, 172, 173, 174, 194
k. Always has high self-esteem until failure mounts	7, 51, 97, 109, 112, 118, 124
l. Doesn't like to listen to explanations – will assure you he knows what to do	38, 52, 53, 54, 86, 87, 118
m. Tells you his errors are never his fault	117, 153, 199

Profile

V. FRIEDA FRIENDLESS – The child with social difficulties

CHARACTERISTICS	STRATEGIES
a. Doesn't participate with other children	96, 125, 131, 133, 134, 135, 136, 138, 145, 146, 153, 154
b. Has no close friends at school	96, 116, 125, 133, 134, 135, 138, 145, 146, 154
c. Is shy	18, 26, 32, 61, 96, 97, 116, 125, 133, 134, 135, 136, 138, 145, 146, 149, 154, 169, 170
d. May be the brunt of other children's jokes	133, 134, 135, 136, 138, 145, 154
e. Misperceives social situations	133, 136, 138, 145, 153, 199
f. Lacks motivation	18, 22, 26, 33, 34, 35, 62, 74, 116, 134, 137, 139, 146
g. Has the "black cloud over the head" syndrome	18, 35, 62, 116, 134, 135, 138
h. Likes to hide in the room	1, 22, 61, 62, 96, 97, 145, 170
i. Uses tiny printing or handwriting	18, 20, 22, 26, 27, 31, 35
j. May display inappropriate interactions in social situations	136, 138, 153, 193, 199

Profile

VI. VIRGINIA VISUAL – The child with visual difficulties

CHARACTERISTICS	STRATEGIES
a. Can't understand written directions but can understand directions when given orally	1, 3, 4, 5, 6, 8, 9, 10, 11, 16, 43, 46, 93, 101, 109, 123, 126, 155, 156, 196
b. Often needs auditory clues to sound out a word, remember letters, or write out numerals	126, 151, 155, 167, 178
c. Makes many reversals: sees and/or writes *p* as *q*, *b* as *d*, *was* as *saw*, etc.	126, 144, 151, 155, 157, 158, 176, 177, 178
d. Has to read aloud for a clear understanding	2, 4, 126, 151, 156, 198
e. Has difficulty keeping her place in reading or number work	45, 72, 126, 151, 177, 178
f. Has difficulty drawing a line between two borders	44, 126, 143, 151, 158, 167, 168, 176, 177, 178
g. Has difficulty in figure-ground activities: can't distinguish a particular form from its background	126, 151, 158, 168, 176, 177, 178
h. Has trouble with hidden pictures	126, 151, 158, 168, 176, 177, 178
i. Has trouble with directionality – up-down, over-under, front-back, left-right	4, 126, 151, 167, 168, 176, 177, 178
j. Has difficulty writing words or letters between proper lines	27, 31, 44, 126, 143, 148, 151, 168
k. Can't start to write unless a sample is given	109, 123, 126, 151
l. Has difficulty recognizing a word if its size, color, or position is changed	16, 126, 144, 151, 176, 177, 178
m. Can't put a picture story in sequence even if the correct sequence is given orally	8, 126, 151, 157, 167, 168
n. Often writes numbers or letters out of sequence, as *brid* for *bird, 91* for *19, 432* for *4302, dring* or *brnig* for *bring*	45, 126, 144, 151, 157, 167, 168, 176, 177, 178

(Continued)

Profile

VI. VIRGINIA VISUAL – The child with visual difficulties (contd.)

CHARACTERISTICS	STRATEGIES
o. Has trouble with puzzles, mazes, dot-to-dot	126, 151, 158, 167, 168, 176, 177, 178
p. Doesn't space properly between numbers, letters	27, 44, 45, 90, 123, 143, 144, 151
q. Has difficulty making particular letters or numbers	27, 44, 45, 90, 123, 144, 176, 178

Profile

VII. SICKLY STUART – The child who uses illness as an avoidance technique

CHARACTERISTICS	STRATEGIES
a. Has frequent stomach aches, headaches	1, 18, 85, 118, 124, 136, 140, 153, 159
b. Always wants to go to the nurse	1, 18, 85, 112, 118, 124, 136, 141, 153, 159
c. Feels sick but doesn't want to go to the nurse	1, 18, 85, 112, 118, 124, 136, 140, 153, 159
d. Often "just doesn't feel good"	1, 18, 112, 118, 124, 136, 141, 153, 159
e. Has to go to the washroom a lot	1, 18, 85, 112, 118, 124, 136, 141, 153, 159
f. Frequently is absent from school	1, 18, 35, 38, 124, 136, 141, 153
g. Spends a lot of time with his head on his desk	1, 18, 22, 23, 38, 42, 43, 59, 74, 76, 105, 136, 153
h. Says his work wasn't done because of his sore finger, his sore foot, his headache, his stomach ache	1, 18, 22, 23, 38, 42, 43, 74, 76, 81, 105, 118, 136, 153
i. Shows evidence of the effects of weather, minor temperatures, full moon, and colds on performance	1, 18, 22, 23, 38, 42, 43, 69, 73, 74, 76, 81, 105, 118, 136, 153
j. May have his parents convinced he truly is often ill	141, 153

Profile

VIII. WILLIE WANTING – The child who needs constant attention

CHARACTERISTICS	STRATEGIES
a. Cries when he gets an answer wrong	18, 43, 51, 115, 116, 118, 132, 136, 146, 147, 153, 157
b. Whines often	18, 62, 67, 85, 111, 112, 115, 118, 131, 132, 136, 147, 153
c. Complains a lot about unjust treatment	105, 113, 115, 136, 147, 153, 194
d. May refuse to do something because supposedly a parent doesn't want him to	85, 115, 117, 118, 124, 132, 136, 147, 153
e. May be selfish with own or school equipment	18, 62, 85, 115, 131, 132, 136, 139, 147, 153, 199
f. Often is a tattletale	85, 111, 112, 113, 115, 131, 132, 136, 147, 153, 199
g. Gets overly distraught if reprimanded	18, 62, 71, 114, 131, 132, 146, 147, 153, 199
h. Cries easily when things are not going exactly the way he wants	18, 62, 112, 115, 132, 136, 146, 147, 153
i. Has an "I won't try unless you're here" attitude	10, 22, 23, 24, 34, 35, 43, 62, 123, 125, 147, 199
j. Uses negative behavior to get attention	1, 23, 29, 59, 60, 61, 62, 63, 64, 65, 66, 67, 70, 85, 111, 112, 115, 118, 132, 136, 139, 147, 153, 194
k. Exhibits a lot of passive aggressive behavior, with explanations such as, "I was just going to sharpen my pencil – his foot was in the way"	1, 60, 63, 64, 65, 70, 112, 118, 132, 136, 139, 147, 153
l. Wants to be physically near the teacher as often as possible	22, 24, 128
m. Asks for help constantly	2, 4, 10, 18, 23, 24, 88, 109, 122, 123, 125, 194, 199

(Continued)

Profile

VIII. WILLIE WANTING – The child who needs constant attention (contd.)

CHARACTERISTICS	STRATEGIES
n. Wants to be pampered	23, 24, 43, 88, 136, 147
o. Often extraordinarily egocentric	115, 132, 153, 193, 199

Profile

IX. AUGIE AUDITORY – The child with auditory difficulties

CHARACTERISTICS	STRATEGIES
a. Can't understand what the teacher says	1, 2, 3, 4, 5, 6, 7, 8, 9, 10, 16, 90, 125, 127, 128, 151, 172, 180, 196
b. Doesn't know what is going on in the classroom	1, 2, 3, 4, 5, 6, 7, 10, 16, 75, 90, 125, 127, 128, 172, 180
c. Complains about the noise in the classroom and lunchroom	1, 2, 3, 4, 5, 6, 16, 75, 128, 172
d. Daydreams a lot	1, 2, 3, 4, 5, 6, 16, 22, 75, 125, 128
e. Needs visual clues to learn letters, words, etc.	2, 16, 17, 22, 90, 151, 166, 167, 172, 179
f. Can't associate a letter sound with a letter in the alphabet	16, 17, 90, 151, 160, 167, 179
g. Learns initial sounds much faster than ending sounds – confuses *hear-heal, pet-pen, five-fire*	16, 17, 151, 160, 167, 179
h. Leaves off word endings in speech	16, 17, 151, 157, 160, 164, 165, 167, 179
i. Omits ending sounds in oral reading	16, 17, 151, 157, 160, 164, 165
j. Is usually a poor speller, and poor in dictation; writes *bend* for *blend, spit* for *split*	17, 18, 22, 121, 151, 167, 179, 200
k. Has difficulty in following oral directions sequentially	1, 2, 3, 4, 5, 6, 8, 10, 17, 22, 46, 90, 125, 128, 151, 172, 180
l. Complains that others talk too much and he never gets a chance to talk	1, 161, 166
m. Has difficulty finishing a sentence; struggles for the proper word	18, 151, 162, 163, 164, 165, 166
n. Wants to participate in show and tell but becomes tongue-tied and is only able to show	18, 139, 151, 162, 163, 164, 165, 166

(Continued)

Profile

IX. AUGIE AUDITORY – The child with auditory difficulties (contd.)

CHARACTERISTICS	STRATEGIES
o. Wants to report on an exciting and interesting event but is unable to continue after the first sentence	151, 162, 163, 164, 165, 166
p. Has a hesitant and choppy oral delivery	151, 162, 163, 164, 165, 166
q. Has trouble rhyming words	17, 18, 151, 165, 167, 179

Profile

X. BEWILDERED BELINDA – The child who has difficulty with organization and concentration

CHARACTERISTICS	STRATEGIES
a. Is extremely distractable	1, 5, 7, 10, 17, 18, 22, 34, 43, 44, 68, 69, 73, 76, 84, 86, 90, 97, 103, 106, 128, 172, 173, 174
b. Loses her place while reading	72, 84, 126, 151, 195
c. Never knows what's going on	2, 7, 8, 9, 18, 22, 29, 30, 34, 35, 40, 43, 46, 49, 51, 52, 68, 69, 73, 74, 76, 84, 88, 95, 97, 99, 104, 105, 109, 120, 122, 123, 128, 172, 173, 174, 195
d. If sent on an errand, forgets where to go before getting there	33, 75, 127, 173
e. Has trouble getting from place to place	29, 33, 40, 75
f. Doesn't have the correct materials	18, 49, 50, 83, 98, 99, 104, 131, 147
g. Produces messy and confusing work	20, 27, 37, 39, 44, 45, 47, 48, 79, 81, 131, 147
h. Loses completed work	36, 41, 42, 43, 50, 74, 79, 81, 83, 131, 147
i. Is confused by a change in routine	30, 40, 199
j. Looks as if she has been run over by a car	82, 129, 131, 147
k. Has a messy desk	36, 50, 83, 131, 147
l. Never erases, just scratches out	20, 37, 44, 47, 48, 79, 80, 81, 131, 147
m. Has trouble getting a task started	2, 8, 43, 46, 76, 195
n. Is a word caller – can read words well but does not comprehend what she is reading	2, 4, 16, 22, 93, 123, 126, 151, 156, 198

(Continued)

41

X. BEWILDERED BELINDA – The child who has difficulty with organization and concentration (contd.)

CHARACTERISTICS	STRATEGIES
o. Often cannot work independently	1, 2, 4, 5, 6, 7, 8, 9, 10, 11, 12, 17, 18, 22, 23, 24, 26, 35, 40, 43, 46, 68, 69, 76, 88, 97, 103, 106, 109, 123, 176, 177, 178
p. Can spend a half hour staring at one problem	2, 8, 16, 22, 23, 46, 76, 90, 101, 105, 109, 199
q. Cannot remember basic arithmetic concepts and processes	12, 13, 22, 23, 46, 90, 101, 123, 126, 151, 157, 160, 168, 181, 185, 187, 189, 190
r. Cannot do math without visual and/or auditory aids	12, 13, 22, 23, 43, 90, 101, 109, 123, 126, 151, 155, 160, 168, 181, 182, 189, 190, 196, 200

SPACEY
TRACY

Profile

XI. SPACEY TRACY – The child with poor retention, short- and long-term

CHARACTERISTICS	STRATEGIES
a. Needs many more explanations than the rest of the class and still may not understand	1, 2, 3, 6, 7, 8, 10, 40, 46, 56, 69, 74, 84, 105, 125, 128, 172, 173, 174, 196
b. Often seems unaware of the fact that she's not keeping up	38, 41, 43, 55, 74, 99, 100, 102, 103, 108, 118, 136, 153, 194
c. Never seems to understand the material	1, 2, 6, 7, 8, 10, 15, 16, 23, 51, 52, 84, 89, 90, 91, 97, 109, 156, 172, 173, 174
d. Has an extremely difficult time with new concepts	2, 7, 8, 10, 12, 51, 84, 107, 108, 122, 125, 126
e. Is usually unaware of current events or the world around her	18, 40, 69, 126, 147, 150
f. Forgets teachers' names	18, 126, 147, 150, 153, 167
g. Sometimes gives answers that have nothing to do with the question	7, 43, 51, 56, 68, 69, 86, 97, 109, 123, 124, 172, 174, 194
h. After explicit directions to use, for example, three colors, will use eight, and then not understand what she did wrong	1, 2, 3, 11, 46, 105, 125, 128, 173, 174, 195
i. Has a great deal of difficulty following through with homework assignments	2, 8, 12, 41, 42, 46, 49, 94, 95, 99, 100, 102, 103, 105, 106, 107, 108, 109
j. Forgets math tables from day to day, hour to hour	13, 14, 15, 16, 45, 89, 91, 107, 122
k. Forgets learned material over vacation, weekends; from day to day, hour to hour	2, 4, 7, 8, 9, 10, 11, 13, 14, 15, 17, 18, 22, 91, 97, 107, 122, 125
l. Gets halfway through an assignment and forgets how to do it	2, 4, 7, 8, 22, 23, 46, 69, 84, 91, 97, 103, 106, 107, 122, 123, 173, 195, 199
m. Forgets gym materials, art supplies	18, 49, 120
n. Forgets basic measuring processes and measurement concepts	13, 91, 92, 122, 126, 168, 188

(Continued)

45

Profile

XI. SPACEY TRACY – The child with poor retention, short- and long-term (contd.)

CHARACTERISTICS	STRATEGIES
o. Cannot tell time, count out money or make change, estimate time or distance, or understand place value	12, 13, 22, 23, 90, 123, 126, 151, 157, 160, 168, 181, 186, 187, 188, 190
p. Cannot relate one math concept to another	12, 13, 22, 23, 89, 90, 126, 151, 157, 160, 168, 181, 190
q. Consistently regroups incorrectly in addition or subtraction	12, 13, 22, 23, 43, 89, 90, 101, 123, 126, 151, 157, 160, 168, 181, 182, 190, 200
r. Cannot get the steps in order in multiplication or division	8, 13, 15, 123, 125, 151, 200

FUMBLE FINGERS FRED

XII. FUMBLE FINGERS FRED – The child with fine motor coordination difficulties

CHARACTERISTICS	STRATEGIES
a. Holds a pencil with other than the thumb and index finger	148, 151, 152, 158
b. Clenches crayons, pencils, chalk	10, 142, 148, 151, 152, 158
c. Presses hard with a pencil	142, 148, 151, 158
d. Writes with his head drooped	18, 147, 148, 151
e. Makes all letters the same height	18, 20, 44, 143, 144, 150, 151
f. Has difficulty making particular letters or numbers	27, 45, 90, 123, 144, 148, 150, 151, 158
g. Dislikes writing	18, 148, 150, 151, 197
h. Fails to finish handwriting assignments	12, 18, 147, 148, 150, 151
i. Can't hold scissors, or holds them awkwardly	148, 150, 151, 152, 158, 167
j. Cuts sloppy, uneven lines	148, 150, 151, 152, 158, 167
k. Can't move the paper while cutting	148, 150, 151, 152, 158, 167
l. Colors with heavy, erratic lines; is unable to keep within the outline	148, 150, 151, 158, 167, 168
m. Has difficulty in handling books, materials, papers; seems to have "butterfingers" or be "all thumbs"	148, 149, 151
n. Is slow with and has difficulty with clothing – buttoning, tying shoelaces, putting on boots, etc.	129, 148, 149, 151
o. Produces illegible written work; demonstrates slow and difficult execution of any assignment	12, 34, 106, 110, 148, 151, 197
p. Can't trace well	148, 150, 151, 152, 158, 167, 168
q. Is clumsy in holding paint brushes, using paste or glue	148, 151, 152, 158, 167

Profile

XIII. TONGUE TWISTER TOM – The child who has trouble with verbal expression

CHARACTERISTICS	STRATEGIES
a. Can't repeat simple directions	1, 2, 3, 4, 5, 6, 7, 8, 9, 10, 11, 35, 44, 46, 52, 105, 109, 123, 126, 128, 151, 156, 172, 173, 174
b. Can't follow simple oral directions	1, 2, 3, 4, 5, 6, 7, 8, 9, 10, 11, 35, 44, 46, 52, 105, 109, 123, 126, 128, 151, 156, 172, 173, 174
c. Has a limited vocabulary	4, 5, 7, 11, 26, 52, 126, 151, 156, 167, 170, 171, 172, 173, 174
d. Has trouble with directionality: up-down, in-out, left-right	4, 5, 126, 151, 165, 166, 167, 170, 171, 172, 173, 174
e. Has difficulty saying a simple sentence	6, 7, 25, 30, 52, 126, 145, 146, 151, 156, 161, 162, 163, 164, 166, 170, 171, 174
f. Uses poor grammar – incorrect prepositions, verbs, pronouns, etc.	7, 25, 52, 126, 151, 156, 164, 165, 166, 170, 171, 172, 174
g. Has a hesitant and uneven oral delivery	7, 25, 26, 30, 52, 126, 138, 146, 147, 151, 156, 161, 162, 163, 164, 165, 166, 170, 171
h. Exhibits heavy breathing, slobbering, etc.	126, 138, 145, 146, 151, 161, 162, 163, 164, 165, 166
i. Refuses to speak to the class	6, 7, 18, 25, 26, 52, 126, 138, 145, 146, 147, 151, 162, 164, 165, 166, 170, 171, 172
j. Uses a lot of "I don't know's" and body language	7, 18, 26, 30, 52, 126, 138, 145, 146, 151, 161, 162, 164, 165, 166, 170, 171, 172
k. Wants to report an exciting and interesting event but is unable to continue after the first sentence	151, 162, 163, 164, 165, 166

BECKY BACKGROUND

Profile

XIV. BECKY BACKGROUND – Past and present influences outside school

CHARACTERISTICS	STRATEGIES
a. Parental pressure	
b. Family conflicts	
c. Cultural problems	
This child fits any of the previous 13 profiles, especially Sarah Silent, Neal Know-It-All, Frieda Friendless, Sickly Stuart, Willy Wanting, and Spacey Tracy.	See strategies for profiles listed. Strategies 113, 114, 116, 119, and 193 especially apply here.

You will often encounter difficulty with parental cooperation, especially in the areas of:

viewing the child realistically as to strengths and weaknesses

lack of consistency in home follow-through

putting blame on the school and teachers

interference with the way the child is being taught

Common Solutions for the Uncommon Child (5 – 8)

The 11 profiles in this section are extensions and combinations of the previous profiles. As the child becomes older, specific learning problems are often masked by outward behavioral difficulties. At times it may be helpful to investigate a child's earlier learning problems and to use the K – 4 profiles in combination with the 5 – 8 profiles.

Profile

I. CARL CONFUSED – The child who cannot process oral or written directions

CHARACTERISTICS	STRATEGIES
a. Misinterprets oral directions	1, 2, 4, 5, 6, 7, 8, 9, 10, 11, 16, 17, 18, 22, 43, 46, 52, 109, 123, 125, 128, 172, 173, 195, 196
b. Misinterprets written directions	1, 2, 3, 4, 5, 6, 7, 8, 9, 10, 11, 16, 18, 22, 42, 46, 52, 55, 93, 101, 109, 123, 125, 173, 195, 196
c. Is unable to read the words in the directions, but can understand directions if given orally	1, 3, 4, 5, 6, 8, 9, 10, 11, 16, 43, 46, 93, 101, 109, 123, 128, 195, 198
d. Is unable to assimilate words of oral or written directions	1, 2, 3, 4, 5, 6, 7, 8, 9, 10, 11, 16, 17, 23, 43, 46, 52, 55, 101, 123, 128, 172, 180, 198
e. Starts out following the correct directions, but gets off the track or completely forgets them halfway through the assignment	1, 2, 3, 5, 6, 7, 8, 9, 10, 11, 17, 18, 23, 43, 46, 52, 68, 97, 109, 173
f. Cannot work independently	1, 2, 4, 5, 6, 7, 8, 9, 10, 11, 12, 17, 18, 22, 23, 24, 26, 35, 40, 43, 46, 68, 69, 76, 88, 97, 103, 106, 109, 123, 195
g. Can't prepare science experiments or class projects without aid	2, 7, 8, 10, 11, 12, 34, 46, 91, 92, 97, 123, 125
h. Has a great deal of difficulty following through with homework assignments	2, 8, 12, 41, 42, 46, 49, 94, 95, 99, 100, 102, 103, 105, 106, 107, 108, 109
i. Can spend a half hour staring at one problem	8, 22, 23, 46, 76, 90, 101, 105, 109, 181
j. Can assemble everything needed for a science experiment, but doesn't know what to do next	2, 3, 6, 8, 10, 11, 46, 97, 123, 125

RICHIE RUSHER

Profile

II. RICHIE RUSHER – The child who rushes through assignments

CHARACTERISTICS	STRATEGIES
a. Generally is careless with any assignment	1, 2, 4, 20, 23, 37, 43, 44, 47, 51, 52, 53, 54, 55, 57, 58, 65, 79, 81, 86, 97, 109, 123, 157, 192
b. Consistently hands in incorrect assignments and incorrect corrections	15, 20, 23, 37, 51, 52, 53, 54, 55, 56, 57, 58, 79, 81, 86, 97, 105, 109, 123, 157, 192, 194
c. Answers questions without reading the material, and then corrects wrong guesses until the answers are correct by chance	7, 20, 37, 51, 52, 53, 54, 55, 56, 57, 58, 79, 81, 86, 105, 192, 198
d. Rushes through tests without reading questions and answers	7, 51, 86, 101, 136, 153, 157, 192
e. Always has very high self-esteem until failure mounts	7, 51, 97, 109, 112, 116, 124, 136
f. Gives illogical verbal and written answers	7, 43, 51, 97, 109, 123, 124, 194
g. Doesn't like to listen to explanations – will assure you he knows what to do	38, 52, 53, 54, 86, 87, 118, 192, 194
h. May be doing an assignment in class the day that it is due	38, 65, 102, 118, 192
I. Research assignments may be totally or partially plagiarized	81, 102, 118, 132, 192

FLIGHTY FLORA

Profile

III. FLIGHTY FLORA – The easily distracted child

CHARACTERISTICS	STRATEGIES
a. Is extremely distractable	1, 5, 7, 10, 17, 18, 22, 34, 43, 44, 68, 69, 73, 76, 84, 86, 90, 94, 97, 103, 106, 128, 137
b. Loses her place while reading	72, 84, 160
c. Never knows what's going on	2, 7, 8, 9, 18, 22, 29, 30, 34, 35, 40, 43, 46, 49, 51, 52, 68, 69, 73, 74, 76, 84, 88, 95, 97, 99, 104, 105, 109, 120, 122, 123, 128
d. Is never in her seat	60, 65, 66, 70, 73, 76, 85, 112, 114, 118, 130
e. Is sensitive to reprimand	59, 71, 85, 114
f. Talks out	59, 60, 65, 66, 85, 112, 114, 118, 137
g. Sometimes gives answers that have nothing to do with the question	7, 43, 51, 56, 68, 86, 97, 109, 123, 124, 172, 174, 194
h. Has trouble getting from place to place	29, 33, 40, 75
i. If sent on an errand, forgets where to go before getting there	33, 75, 127, 169, 180, 194
j. Shows evidence of the effects of weather, minor temperatures, full moon, and colds on performance	30, 43, 44, 69, 73, 97, 110
k. Doesn't take schoolwork as seriously as she could	102, 118, 153, 192

LAZY LARRY

Profile

IV. LAZY LARRY – The child capable of grade level achievement but poorly motivated

CHARACTERISTICS	STRATEGIES
a. Understands assignments but doesn't use class time	1, 22, 23, 38, 42, 53, 58, 69, 85, 97, 99, 102, 105, 118, 131, 192
b. Rarely completes assignments on time	38, 42, 53, 85, 99, 100, 102, 105, 118, 192
c. Never does homework	38, 42, 53, 85, 99, 100, 102, 105, 118 192
d. Daydreams	1, 38, 69, 85, 96, 97, 105, 112, 118
e. Often complains that school is boring and stupid	85, 105, 111, 115
f. Usually shifts the blame for work not done to someone or something else	38, 102, 105, 117, 118, 124, 194
g. Often hands in half-done assignments	38, 42, 53, 58, 81, 85, 86, 99, 100, 105, 118, 192
h. Would always rather do a different assignment from the one that is assigned	38, 42, 81, 85, 102, 105, 118
i. Never feels like working "today"	38, 42, 81, 85, 102, 105, 118
j. Makes statements like: "Couldn't I just do four [out of eight]?" "Why do I have to use complete sentences?" "I can't help it if I didn't understand it."	38, 42, 85, 87, 102, 105, 118
k. May be a master at getting answers instead of help from classmates, parents, teachers	191, 192
l. May copy research assignments	81, 118, 132, 191, 192

DAVE DISTRACTOR

Profile

V. DAVE DISTRACTOR – The classroom distractor

CHARACTERISTICS	STRATEGIES
a. Uses negative behavior to get attention	1, 23, 29, 59, 60, 61, 62, 63, 64, 65, 66, 67, 70, 85, 111, 112, 115, 118, 131, 132, 136, 153
b. Picks fights	1, 29, 60, 61, 62, 63, 65, 66, 67, 70, 85, 112, 113, 132, 136, 153
c. Is satisfied with negative attention	1, 29, 59, 60, 61, 62, 63, 64, 65, 66, 67, 70, 85, 112, 132, 135, 153, 194
d. Is never in his seat	1, 29, 59, 60, 61, 62, 63, 64, 65, 66, 67, 85, 97, 111, 112, 118, 130, 131, 132, 136, 153
e. Is the class clown	1, 29, 59, 60, 61, 62, 63, 64, 65, 66, 67, 70, 85, 97, 111, 112, 113, 114, 118, 131, 132, 136, 153
f. Talks out	1, 29, 59, 60, 61, 62, 63, 64, 65, 66, 67, 85, 97, 111, 112, 114, 118, 132, 136, 153, 194
g. Exhibits a lot of passive aggressive behavior, with explanations such as, "I was just going to sharpen my pencil – his foot was in the way"	1, 60, 63, 64, 65, 70, 112, 118, 132
h. Makes noises, sounds, grimaces, often to no one in particular	111, 118, 132, 136, 195

Profile

VI. MESSY MISSA – The organizational problem child

CHARACTERISTICS	STRATEGIES
a. Doesn't have correct materials	18, 49, 50, 83, 98, 99, 104
b. Has trouble getting a task started	2, 8, 43, 46, 76, 180, 181
c. Produces messy and confusing work	20, 27, 37, 39, 44, 45, 47, 48, 79, 81, 194, 197
d. Loses completed work	36, 41, 42, 43, 50, 74, 79, 81, 83
e. Uses the wrong side of paper	21, 44, 77, 78, 79, 81
f. Never erases, just scratches out	20, 37, 44, 47, 48, 79, 80, 81, 194
g. Is confused by a change of routine	30, 40
h. Forgets notes and materials at home or forgets them at school	18, 36, 49, 50, 83, 98
i. Looks as if she has been run over by a car	82
j. Always has a messy desk	36, 50, 83
k. Always has a messy locker	98
l. Can't take or keep notes	36, 50, 91, 104, 109, 122, 123
m. Always has messy notebooks	36, 98, 104, 192, 194
n. Never seems to have a pencil or clean paper	98, 104, 120
o. Can't seem to build from one method to the next, especially with math sequences	15, 52, 91, 95, 107, 109, 122, 126, 151, 160, 181, 200
p. Rarely attends review sessions or pursues extra help	13, 91, 107, 122, 151, 160, 181, 192

(Continued)

83

Profile

VI. MESSY MISSA – The organizational problem child (contd.)

Characteristics	*Strategies*
q. May look totally blank in response to direct questions, either about work or behavior	128, 195, 199, 194
r. May leave school or home with the correct books/assignments in hand or bag, but mysteriously loses them en route	49, 120, 150, 199, 194

Profile

VII. CLASSIC CLARENCE – The slow learner (who tries like heck)

CHARACTERISTICS	STRATEGIES
a. Always has a confused look	1, 2, 6, 7, 8, 10, 16, 23, 51, 52, 89, 90, 91, 95, 97, 151, 157, 160, 168, 180, 181
b. Is always in for help	2, 10, 16, 51, 52, 89, 90, 91, 97, 151, 157, 168
c. Never seems to understand material	1, 2, 6, 7, 8, 10, 16, 23, 51, 52, 89, 90, 91, 97, 160, 174, 200
d. Consistently does poorly on tests	2, 14, 101, 110, 122, 151, 157
e. Rarely finishes tests	2, 51, 101, 110, 157
f. Can't use reference materials	10, 107, 125, 126, 151
g. Can't rephrase information	6, 10, 122, 125, 126, 171, 174
h. Has an extremely difficult time with new concepts	2, 7, 8, 10, 12, 51, 107, 122, 125, 126, 151, 160, 168, 181
i. Can stare at one problem for 45 minutes and be no further along than he was at the beginning	2, 7, 8, 10, 12, 23, 34, 97, 103, 106, 107, 122, 125, 126, 160, 181
j. Needs numerous explanations for understanding	2, 3, 6, 7, 8, 10, 22, 23, 122, 125, 151

Profile

VIII. ZERO ZELDA – The low self-image child

CHARACTERISTICS	*STRATEGIES*
a. Tears up work before completed	10, 18, 22, 23, 34, 43, 106, 125, 192
b. Often says "I can't"	2, 6, 10, 22, 23, 34, 35, 43, 106, 125, 131, 133, 134, 180
c. Has an "I won't try unless you're here" attitude	10, 22, 23, 24, 34, 35, 123, 125
d. Is afraid to speak up in class even if her answer is correct	18, 25, 26, 35, 116, 161, 164, 170, 171
e. Has poorly developed motor skills	20, 22, 27, 31, 35, 126
f. Uses tiny printing or handwriting	20, 22, 27, 31, 35, 126
g. Avoids eye contact	28, 32, 35, 61, 171
h. Hardly ever completes assignments because they are wrong (she thinks, anyway)	10, 18, 22, 23, 34, 35, 53, 62, 106, 109, 123, 133, 181, 192
i. Is sluggish – lags in hallway or doesn't care if she is late	29, 33, 35, 62
j. Has the "black cloud over the head" syndrome	18, 35, 62, 116, 135
k. Lacks motivation	18, 22, 26, 33, 34, 35, 62, 74, 116, 135
l. Is absent a lot, looks asleep	22, 30, 33, 35
m. Likes to hide in the room	1, 22, 61, 62, 96, 97
n. Resists help	22, 23, 97, 107, 122, 126
o. Won't seek help before or after school or during class time	97, 107, 122, 126, 160, 192

Profile

IX. SALLY WHO? – The child with poor retention, short- and long-term

CHARACTERISTICS	STRATEGIES
a. Forgets directions	2, 3, 4, 5, 6, 7, 8, 9, 10, 11, 18a, 22, 46, 70, 88, 94, 97, 109, 123, 125, 128, 172, 173, 180, 196
b. Forgets math tables (addition and multiplication) and basic processes (carrying and borrowing), even when introduced each year	13, 14, 15, 16, 45, 89, 91, 107, 122, 160, 181, 200
c. Forgets learned material over vacation, weekends; from day to day, even morning to afternoon	2, 4, 7, 8, 9, 10, 11, 13, 14, 15, 17, 18, 22, 91, 97, 107, 122, 125, 160, 181
d. Forgets or confuses the class schedule	18, 29, 30, 40, 173, 189
e. Can't remember time of day or day of the week	18, 29, 30, 170, 173, 184
f. Gets halfway through assignments and forgets how to do them	2, 4, 7, 8, 22, 23, 46, 69, 84, 91, 97, 103, 106, 107, 122, 123, 173, 181
g. Forgets gym materials, art supplies	49, 120
h. Does poorly on tests	2, 6, 8, 93, 101, 107, 110, 122
i. Can't do basic measuring processes	13, 91, 92, 122, 126, 151
j. Can't spell simple words	121, 122, 151
k. Forgets simple grammar rules	91, 92, 107, 122, 126, 151, 168
l. Has extreme difficulty with the spelling book	2, 6, 51, 56, 97, 102, 103, 109, 121, 123, 151

FLIRTY GERTIE

Profile

X. FLIRTY GERTIE – The social butterfly

CHARACTERISTICS	STRATEGIES
a. Can't concentrate on work because of preoccupation with the opposite sex	1, 18, 22, 23, 35, 42, 53, 59, 60, 62, 68, 74, 111, 112, 116, 117, 118, 137
b. Is constantly talking	1, 18, 22, 23, 35, 53, 59, 60, 62, 68, 111, 112, 115, 118, 132
c. Performs below potential	18, 42, 53, 60, 74, 97, 100, 118, 122
d. Doesn't complete assignments	18, 23, 35, 42, 53, 62, 74, 81, 97, 99, 100, 102, 108, 117, 118, 132, 192
e. Knows what's going on with every person in the school	59, 60, 62, 68, 111, 112, 115, 118
f. Often whispering or passing notes	81, 111, 118, 132, 136, 195
g. Clothing may be inappropriate	20, 82, 136, 193

BECKY BACKGROUND

Profile

XI. BECKY BACKGROUND – Past and present influences outside school

CHARACTERISTICS	STRATEGIES
a. Parental pressure	
b. Family conflicts	
c. Cultural problems	

This child fits any of the previous 10 profiles, especially Richie Rusher, Flighty Flora, Lazy Larry, Dave Distractor, Zero Zelda, and Flirty Gertie.

See strategies for profiles listed. Strategies 113, 114, 116, 119, and 193 especially apply here.

You will often encounter difficulty with parental cooperation, especially in the areas of:

viewing the child realistically as to strengths and weaknesses

lack of consistency in home follow-through

putting blame on the school and teachers

interference with the way the child is being taught

STRATEGIES

Strategies

1. Have the child sit in the front of the room, near the teacher.

2. Have the child repeat directions to see if he understands them.

3. Have another student or teacher read the directions to the child.

4. Make sure the child understands word meanings:

    a. individual main words, for example, *summarize*
    b. function words, for example, *between* vs. *beside*

5. If using longer words, use simpler synonyms that the child might be familiar with; the repetition of the concept in more than one way is less redundant than repeating the same confusing directions over and over again.

6. Have the child rephrase the directions in his own words.

7. Monitor the child's work, ask him to show you what he has done when half completed, and have him explain what he is doing.

8. Break down the directions into a sequence of steps; number the steps, and have the child complete the task one step at a time.

9. Use short, complete sentences, especially when giving oral directions, and pause after the delivery of each idea; avoid run-on sentences and ones that may sound too long.

10. Utilize an academically stable student to help monitor this child's work or to help explain directions to him.

11. Be more visual in giving directions; show the children exactly what will be expected of them.

12. Shorten assignments.

13. Use the recess period once a week to brush up on basic math facts.

14. Before each math lesson, put problems on the chalkboard to reinforce carrying and borrowing procedures; do this every day for only five minutes.

15. Make sure to analyze the errors in the child's work; be sure you know why the child is making the errors.

16. Use the chalkboard more, especially for auditorily oriented children who need a visual as well as auditory cue.

17. Use indoor recess to utilize many kinds of listening games to help children to improve skills.

18. Make check lists that the child can use to denote his personal program:

    a. following directions correctly
    b. classroom schedule
    c. assignment completion
    d. image builder (special stars or marks for every time the child speaks up)
    e. organization lists (materials needed for a specific subject)
    f. staying in his seat
    g. not talking

19. Give the child a piece of paper for the assignment and a piece of paper to doodle on, or to tear up.

20. Set strict standards on assignment appearances, and stick to them.

21. Mark the correct side of the paper with a small red x and have the child mark the rest of his papers himself.

22. Check the child's work frequently; don't stay at your desk while the children work; walk around and spread encouragement.

23. Have the child do two or three problems with you, tell him to do two on his own, and then say you will be back to check his work.

24. Explain to the child that he cannot monopolize all your time, that you understand his plight and will try to give him as much time as you can, but that he must be patient.

25. Don't force the child to answer if he doesn't want to, even if you know he has the right answer.

26. Have the child tell you the answer, and then relate it to the rest of the class by saying, "Chris gave the correct answer, which is _____"; always give the child verbal credit.

27. Require the child to write large; say you want to see the tall letters reach from the bottom to the top of the line; ask the child to skip lines between work; say it will make it easier for you to read his good work.

28. Set the example yourself and use lots of direct eye contact; mention the child's beautiful eyes.

29. When the children line up, put this child in the front or close to the front of the line so he doesn't lag behind.

30. Ask the child occasionally what time it is, or what subject he has next.

31. With written work, require the child to fill the whole line.

32. Encourage eye contact with games, such as "stare me down for 15 seconds," etc.

33. Time the child to see how long it takes to get from place to place.

34. Have the child do a shortened version of class projects.

35. Give verbal rewards for being on time, handing in neat work, getting work in on time.

36. Organize the child's desk with marked file folders.

37. Never accept messy work.

38. Always be consistent in terms of assignments – when they must be done, and quality that will be accepted.

39. Make sure that all corrections are turned in on a separate sheet of paper.

40. Make sure the child has a guardian angel (another student) to help him get through a day when the routine is changed.

41. Have the child turn in work as soon as it is completed.

42. Never let late work extend further than one day if possible; have the child do it during recess or free time, if necessary.

43. Have the child check with you when half the work is completed to make sure he is doing it correctly; compliment him when it is.

44. Show the child how to organize his work; you do an example, pointing out how one should space words, skip lines between answers, etc.

45. Use graph paper for complicated math work; make sure the child puts one number in each box.

46. Write down the steps needed to do an assignment.

47. Explain how to use an eraser and why the child must use it.

48. Make sure the child only uses pencil for math work; only God can use a pen when He does math work, for He makes no mistakes.

49. Make a check list for the child of material that is to go home; get a parent to sign it, if possible.

50. Help the child to clean out his desk at least twice a week.

51. Monitor the child closely to be sure he isn't putting down just any answer.

52. When the child finishes an assignment, ask him to tell you the main idea of the work or to explain the process that he used.

53. Have the child do all corrections during recess or free time.

54. Explain that it is always easier to do it right the first time rather than doing it again on his own time.

55. Don't allow the child to do more than one assignment at a time unless it is checked.

56. If the child consistently errs, analyze the errors to see if he actually reads the material.

57. Ask the child why he is always in a rush; find out why.

58. If you are sure the child understands the work but continues to be inaccurate or messy, make him do it again and again; do this a couple of times and he will get the message.

59. Ignore disruptive behavior if possible; compliment the child with a verbal and physical gesture when he is behaving appropriately.

60. Isolate the child's desk, but remember that he is there when he is not being disruptive.

61. Use direct eye contact whenever talking to the child.

62. Give the child a special project when he behaves well.

63. Direct the children in the class when this child is out of the room that his antics are not appropriate and that you need their assistance to help him control his behavior.

64. Never fly off the handle; this child lives off the teacher's frustrations.

65. Don't give the child an inch; always be consistent.

66. Find positive consequences for the child to develop the desire to be good.

67. Say that you will not tolerate the child's disruptive behavior.

68. Don't let the child converse away from the subject at any time, especially in independent work times; he can speak only of math at math time, etc.

69. Say the child's name once in a while to see what he is doing.

70. For a particularly disruptive student, sit next to him and use some sort of physical contact to calm him down; help him with his work.

71. Don't worry about bruising his sensitive nature; this child forgets quickly and rarely carries a grudge.

72. Give the child a place keeper for reading work.

73. Have patience with the child when he is under the weather.

74. Have check lists to be used when work is completed.

75. If the child goes on an errand, make sure he has easy instructions for what he is to do.

76. Time the child for getting started – "10 seconds to get your name on the paper."

77. Throw away assignments that are on the wrong side of the paper – but give warning before doing this.

78. Have the child recopy the assignment (on his own time) to the correct side.

79. Have the child redo the complete assignment.

80. Don't accept scratch-outs – the child must erase and correct.

81. Keep the child after school or during recess to redo assignments – if you keep him one or two times until the assignment is complete, he will know you mean business.

82. Compliment the child when he does look nice.

83. Dump the child's desk on the floor after school – make him go through and clean up the materials.

84. Adjust the assignment for the child's short attention span.

85. Make the child follow classroom rules as everyone else.

86. Set a limit as to how many errors will be accepted; better yet, say how many correct responses you expect (make sure the child understands the assignment first).

87. If work is incorrect because the child rushes through it, set up consequences and tell him in advance:

    a. "You need to get 8 of these 10 problems correct or you will redo them all."
    b. "You need to get 16 out of 20 correct or you will write out complete sentences during recess."

88. Limit the number of questions the child can ask about written or oral directions.

89. Allow the use of a math grid for tables.

90. Give visual examples, especially for math.

91. Have the child construct a notebook, with only formulas and examples.

92. Keep a teacher-made reference notebook in class.

93. Have another student read tests to the child.

94. Have the child divide long-term assignments into sections; set a due date for each section.

95. Check with other teachers and compare subject matter that will transfer from one class to the next. Keep teaching strategies similar – such as using metrics in science and math.

96. Don't allow the child to isolate himself in the classroom.

97. Try to check on the child from time to time.

98. Have the child clean his locker regularly.

99. Require the child to keep a daily assignment sheet.

100. Have the parents sign the daily assignment sheet.

101. Allow the child to take the test in the resource room.

102. Keep the child after school that night for incomplete assignments (this can be prearranged with most parents – they are cooperative).

103. Allow the child to do every other problem.

104. Have the child keep organized folders – one for each subject.

105. Make sure this child in particular knows exactly what is expected of him and when it's due.

106. If possible, cut the child's assignments, but make sure he sticks to the agreed-upon cut.

107. Invite the child in to a morning or afternoon session to show concern; possibly involve the parents by calling them about such a session.

108. Check to make sure the child's assignment is written down in a good place.

109. When the child begins the assignment, check to be sure he's on the right track.

110. Give the child extra time on a test.

111. Say something like, "I personally do not care for behavior of this sort in my room. Please reserve it for elsewhere."

112. Put things in black and white – a certain type of behavior will be accepted, and that's it.

113. In the area of values, use statements such as, "Tell me how you would feel if it happened to you."

114. Say, "I care for you as a person. Though I may not like the things you do, I still care for you as a person."

115. Make statements such as, "It seems to me you did or said _____ because you want my attention (other students' attention)."

116. Make statements such as, "I see this is something you are good at."

117. Refuse to let the child play the shift-the-blame game; state facts or call him on it; if he says, "My mother said _____" or "Mrs. _____ said _____," then say, "When I talk to _____ this afternoon, I will ask her if that is what she said."

118. State expected short-term behavior and consequences; always follow through and always be consistent.

119. With parents, state facts – if possible, never voice an opinion.

120. Send notes home about materials needed.

121. Work with the resource teacher about setting up a special spelling program.

122. Have a review session to which you invite the child.

123. Give the child an example of what he is to do.

124. If possible, have frequent brief conversations with the child so he knows he can't play parent against teacher.

125. Ask another student, whom the child likes, to help him.

126. Ask the resource room teacher to work on a specific concept, such as main idea, summarizing, the paragraph, or a particular math concept.

127. Make sure errands are clearly written out, and/or understood by child.

128. Stand by the child's desk as often as possible when talking to the class.

129. Keep a check list that shows how many times the child comes in totally dressed.

130. Give the child specific times that he may get up out of his seat.

131. Send complimentary notes home when the child's behavior is appropriate and/or improving.

132. Don't let yourself react emotionally to the child's inappropriate behavior; cite the behavior you see him exhibiting; tell him other choices he has in the area of behavior; tell him the behavior that you expect of him and that he should expect of himself.

133. Give this child and another child a project to do together outside the classroom – it is sometimes easier to be friendly without 25 others around.

134. If possible, arrange special project times for the child in the room or with a special or resource teacher – sometimes alone, sometimes with other children.

135. Try to arrange some "alone time" for the child – even three or four minutes with you.

136. Try to talk openly and honestly with the child about some of his behaviors. Venture some guesses as to how you might see it from his point of view – many times he will respond.

137. Pat the child's shoulder as you walk by his desk; touch him lightly on the arm if you want his attention – in a small group.

138. Talk with the resource teacher about involving the child in some small-group non-academic activities.

139. Find out from the parents what the child likes to do at home, and work out a project he could do and bring to school.

140. Tell the child that if he's sick he has to go to the nurse; if he doesn't want to go to the nurse, then he obviously isn't sick.

141. Discuss the problem with the parents – then explain to the child in long and involved detail that work missed during time spent in the nurse's office, in the washroom, or at home will have to be made up; then follow through.

142. Have the child use a pencil holder or a rubber band.

143. Allow the use of special lined paper.

144. Use finger tracing, possibly with a sandpaper alphabet.

145. Encourage the child to participate in board games and other games in the room – it may help the child feel more relaxed.

146. If possible, arrange a special time with the art teacher; this child may often respond better in this situation than in others.

147. Set up a point system for a specific behavior, using a special project or special times with a favorite teacher as the earned reward.

148. If possible, involve the child in a special P.E. program to work on gross and fine motor difficulties.

149. Make the child a special helper, to carry things, rearrange desks, etc.

150. Talk with the parents – have a check sheet for things the child works on at home, and keep a point sheet at school.

151. Have the resource teacher work on areas of special difficulty.

152. If possible, arrange with the music, art, or P.E. teacher to involve the child in a special activity that would help him improve his skills.

153. When possible, be very frank with the child, pointing out the realities of a given situation – this will need to be done more than once.

154. If possible, try to get one or two of the more understanding students in the class to befriend the child occasionally.

155. Give the child auditory clues, but try to gradually reduce the number of clues you give.

156. Have the child read a phrase silently and then tell you what it said; work up to a sentence, then a paragraph.

157. When the child makes an error, have him go over it and see if he can recognize his error.

158. During indoor recess or free time, try to encourage the child to work with simple puzzles, paper cutting, coloring, mazes, dot-to-dot, block designs, or art activities, either with another child or with you.

159. Find out from the parents if the child really has a physical problem and, if possible, set specific times for him to use the washroom, see the nurse, etc.

160. If possible, keep the child in a small reading or math group in which extra practice could benefit the whole group.

161. Try to watch the child and be aware of when he wants to speak – you may even set up a system with him whereby he can cue you if he wants to say something, and then you cue him as he's speaking (as described in the next strategy).

162. Cue the child with letter sounds or word beginnings when he's speaking to the class.

163. If possible, work with the child in practicing what he wants to say.

164. Have the child read from something written down after he's practiced.

165. Encourage the child to play games which would allow him to speak, rhyme words, use correct grammar.

166. Recommend the child for speech-language services, or ask for suggestions from a speech-language pathologist.

167. Use an occasional indoor recess time to go over areas of difficulty, possibly in game form.

168. Ask the resource teacher for special help worksheets the child could work on in the classroom.

169. Send the child on an errand you are certain he can handle.

170. Have the child tell you what he did last night, over the weekend.

171. Encourage oral language activities.

172. Have the child listen to simple riddles; then ask him to answer them.

173. Encourage simple memory games, with the child actively participating by following directions.

174. Read short stories, followed by questions dealing with the details, sequence, main idea, inferences, and conclusions.

175. Encourage structured activities at recess, such as hopping games, walking a straight line (forwards, backwards, and sideways), ball bouncing, etc.

176. Have the child work on copying geometric figures using rubber bands, cards, blocks, etc.

177. Encourage games such as dominoes, cards, (making suits, pictures, numbers, sets), letter bingo, etc.

178. Encourage games matching, sorting, and tracing letters and words.

179. Use tapes and records of sounds, words, stories, etc.

180. Start by giving simple oral directions, and progress to more difficult ones.

181. Have the child do one or two problems with you each day, involving the difficult process.

182. Use visual aids with the child concurrently with the numerical symbols.

183. Ask the child to count for you.

184. Ask the child occasionally what time it is.

185. Have the child count out real money to you.

186. Discuss prices, distance, and basic measurement with the class, possibly in a social studies or science unit.

187. Let this child and another child drill each other with flash cards.

188. Encourage math games.

189. Have the student keep a daily schedule on his desk.

190. Have very close communication between home and school — notes, phone calls, daily assignment/comment sheets.

191. Arrange a time when you can talk one-to-one with the student so he can explain his work to you.

192. Have the student work in your room during recess, or a special event he doesn't want to miss, to do or redo work.

193. If possible, refer the student to the school counselor, social worker, or psychologist.

194. Teach the student to question herself in regard to behavior and/or finished work.

195. If possible, have the resource teacher or another support person work in your room with you and the student to improve on-task performance.

196. Combine visual, oral and tactile explanations as often as you can.

197. Utilize the computer, either by the student or helpful adult, to help student complete written assignments.

198. Read to, or have a responsible adult read to, the student and have her read the same sentence/passage back to you.

199. Model strategies for the student to approach work/behavior.

200. Utilize the computer to work on areas of difficulty.

GENERAL GUIDELINES FOR TEACHERS

1. Whenever you get frustrated with these children, reread the strategies to get a refreshing approach.

2. Never let a problem go more than two days before contacting the special education teacher or other resource person with whom the student works.

3. Ask the resource person what kind of help the child is receiving in the resource room.

4. If you see an area of need for the child while he is in your class, mention it so that the special education teacher or other resource person can work it into the program.

5. Set your expectancies for these children within their capabilities.

6. If the child does not seem to be catching on with a particular concept, give the special education teacher or other resource person time to work more closely with that child.

7. Try not to let these children get too far behind the rest of the class; this only reinforces their feeling that they are inferior or bad students.

8. If you are having a problem with a specific student, it sometimes helps to make notes on what it is that he is doing and also write down what you are doing about the problem.

9. Be consistent.

10. Have lots of patience for the child who functions poorly when under the weather or preoccupied with other projects.

11. At the start of each year, make a short check list and test of common knowledge precepts: days of week, months of year, time telling, basic measurement.

12. Give a basic math test to find out who can add, subtract, multiply, and divide.

13. Keep lots of appropriate worksheets, games, or assignments for the students who have no work or who have completed their assignments.